Timeless Expressions of a Poet's Mind

Timothy Pond

India | USA | UK

Presentation by *BookLeaf Publishing*

Web: www.bookleafpub.com

E-mail: info@bookleafpub.com

ISBN: 9789363302143

First edition 2024

The Hearts Truths

Within this body beats the heart of a poet
Your pressence and loving soul to me inspire
I looked for someone with a heart as warm as yours
Along the way it had grown cold burned out fire

Then you returned to my life and found my heart
The moment i looked into your eyes i knew it was
fate all along
Like twinkling stars that one was to make a wish
upon
And with each touch with every smile it grew once
more strong

My wish is that forever is in the cards for you and me
We are so much alike soulmates we may have found
With each passing day may you know just as much
That my words are true and for you i wanna always
be around

Once every now and again we shall briefly be apart
Just know that ill be not far just a heart beat away
With open arms and gentle kiss always waiting for
thee
All this forever thanks for accepting my heart that
day

My three Wishes

Three wishes granted upon me
Wish happiness always for me and you
That is if i had three wishes
Pray that this one surely come true

With three wishes what more could i ask
Maybe wish to you my heart is accepted
That is if i had three wishes
And may you with my heart never again rejected

Once more three wishes granted to me
There out of there might only need be one
That is if i had three wishes
For you see you would be my only one

The Power of one

Her loving heart a power to be
Giving all and more never taking away
Since fate brought her to me
It was her that i gave my heart to away

Forever she is in my thoughts
Her image enternally in my heart
She is unlike any one that came before
This was a new begining a whole other start

A heart that is loving unlike any other
Her soul hiding all my fears
It was not her that found him but fate
His heart lost torn now no longer in tears

She reaches forth and takes his hand
Guiding him along the path
A new sensation a feeling felt from deep within
One he was alone now add one you do the math

Her name is that of more than one
But she is just one with the love of the world
He see himself a long time with her
Now an empty heart is now filled with her world

Blessed Gift

I had thought love was oh so gone
Never did somethings feel right
Just as with each sun rise did i try
With each new moon shining bright

Ive finally found someone in my life
She is the one with a heart so giving and kind
She touches my soul and lifts my spirits high
The one who is forever in my heart always on my mind

She has blessed me with her love
Oh how can i begin to tell her how i feel
She has shown me so much is out there
And that true love can be truely real

When she is around my heart and eyes are open
These feelings and more are lifes true key
Realizing all that was once lost
Brought out from deep within me

Shes filled a void a missing peice
Feelings that i once tried to hide
She has touched my heart givin it life
Now i see clearly far and wide
You see i have fallen for this lady
To her i give my all my heart
Each day i dream of her in my arms
I wish and pray that we never part

Her name means more than one
This lady who i give to all my love
To me she has become one of a kind
Truely a blessing a gift from above

What she means to me

5

Each new morning i awake
First thing i reach over for you
Open my eyes to glance at an angel
I see you staring back at me too

Each night you are in my dreams
Through sometimes we are apart
Fate still keeps us close as one
For now you once again have my heart

Time had seperated us for some years
But true love cant be apart forever
I waited for the time but never knew when
But now we are one may nothing ever sever

I find myself with each new day unending
May our feelings and you and i never end
I Pledge to give myself always to you
My heart,my love,to you i eternally send

A Smile Away

Never to the past did i have the chance
Always i felt something was lost
It was the words that the time needed said
My heart was silenced at a cost

Never i thought we would cross paths again
Still today the image of your smile in my mind
Wished that what we have to last forever
One in a million a heart as yours hard to find

Now we have found each one after so long
With you eyes that will never cry
Lips from which never comes untruths
A true strong love that surely never die

Each time im around you my words are slient
Each times you see beauty in my eyes
Its because these eyes are looking at you
What you see is what you get no false truths no lies

Fate brought us forth for a future to reserve
A missed chance to say a simple i love you
I would always miss you even if we never met
Now i give you the words a forever i love you
You know i care when i ask why you crying
Today if a happy smile comes to you
A happy smile that perhaps you cant explain
Its Because At that moment I am thinking of you and
smiling too

Hand For The Future

You are honest,decent and pure heart
Days for you sometimes seem so rough
Life throws you curves your path seem not clear
Its these obstacles that makes one tough

I ask that you let me be your guiding light
Take my hand and let me guide you thru
Together as one but as two can fight
For you see as one ive went thru it too

I give you my heart my being all i can
When things look down i wanna be there to catch
Im just a mere human who wants to be your man
When times seem cold things grow dark let me light a
match

All you see is all real words i share are true
So please you need not runaway nor be afraid
I think you soon from reading this words feel it too
Hand in hand together a future can be made

To Hold Within My Heart

A night of loneliness i'm thinking of you
As i wake up to find that i'm thinking of you
As my mind keeps on turning of the things that are true
It breaks my heart cause i'm missing you

A kiss and some laughter always having a great time
As my day goes by i'm lonely and sad
Im thinking about love that thought was so hard to find
I just want to touch you, it's driving me mad

Its your sense of magic that has brought me closer to you
I express my feelings through letters and words
Always letting you know youcaptured my heart with all the
things that you do
It's nothing my darling that you haven't heard

Im yours and all i have turned by your special touch
Together both there for each others hard times time stand
still
I want you to know that i love you so much
I'll hold that forever baby you know i will

Forever And Always

Whats life like when im with you
Its like forever is just a heartbeat away
For you each day my love continues to grow
Heres to thanks to the heavens sending you my way

Two hearts beating as one so full of love
These precious moments i treasure with my soul
Who truely knows how much i love you
One may never really know

My spirits soar and my heart beats rapidly
Feelings from within ive never felt before
Just even with the slightest touch of your hand
I love and care for you more

Never do i want to say goodbye
The feelings i miss whenever apart
One thing my dear i want you to always know,
Its your pressence forever deep in my heart

With one thing i always want you to remember
A simple set of words to hold true
These words from my heart that is clear
"Forever and always i will love you"

Blessings of You

Not a night doesnt go by i dream of you as the one
As i wake to the new day your image still so clear
Even with things to face ahead for the day its you i see
A tear rolls down my cheek a place missing in my heart

Your smile the sound of your laughter is what brightens my
day
Its what keeps me going when my day seems to gloom
For many a time i thought love was truely hard to find
Untill the day when i met you and my heart began to
beleive

Something never thought possible eminated from you
Its feelings such as these and more that inspire all i write
forth
The words of my writings letting you know youve touched
my soul
Never are they mere words but everlasting impressions

With these and my love i give always to you cherish as you
will
May i be the hand to guide you from falling a shoulder to
cry upon
This and so much more is yours and with these closing
words
Hold within your hand my beating heart in return blessings
of my love

Raindrops of Emotions

Feelings are as small rain drops from heaven
Each falling appearing to dance as comes down
With happiness and sometimes sadness as well
A glimpse of life even if with a frown

Each time i look into your eyes i fall more for you
Now these drops fall merely into one special place
This place where feelings emerge a place you know too
Deep within ones soul where the heart beats spirits race

Each word each line spoken another passing of time
This moment wonderous and so full of wonder and might
I raised my head up and looked with a tear to the sky
Closing my eyes make a wish to the night

I never knew for sure if wishes came true
Soon i knew that sometimes the heart felt ones do
With my tears mixed with the new fallen rain
It wasnt just answered by single raindrops but by you

Thru the Glass Out

Sitting here by the window watching the world outside
Life seems to move at differant paces no same speed
Here looking out not wandering out here i hide
Watching the world grow as watching it from a seed

Day becomes night night once again day
The sunshines sometimes covered by falling rain
But it seems to not slow the moving world down
The raindrops like heavens tears rolling down the window
pane

I was once such as those out filled with life
But for now i sit here watch all what to come about
One day a part of this world i shall once set foot
So till that time my heart stays inside waiting it out

Time mends broken hearts and time heals loves wounds
Good things come to those who wait without doubt
At the end of the day i pull down the shade till next
Ill be once again sitting here looking thru the glass out

To Find a Soulmate

Each day spent with you my heart shines
Brighter than the night sky with all the stars
Deep within comes laughter thought long gone
The words of a poet has meaning with no previous scars

The music of angels ring thru your voice your every word
Time with you seems never at a stand still but flows
gradualy
The world and all that is i can see for the beauty shows
Happiness fills my pen and the words free no long in
captivity

At night i dream of nothing more than to be holding you
Anticipation of the day to come when your smile i can see
The doors of heaven opened wide and one of its own fell
As if a sign the many nights of praying an angel just for me

Never shall you feel alone as i to once was for now we are
one
Let us sit side by side and watch the sun rise upon the
oceans side
With a simple smile i know that with you there hopely
never an end
To you i shall reveal all that is me and never a secret shall i
hide

I give you my all my soul the being of who i am and more
You fuel this fire that burns within my heart each firey beat
Take my hand and walk with me together maybe could be
forever
My hearts search for the one to call soulmate is finally
complete

Loves Hidden Quicksand

The journey of the heart begins
The path it takes is sometimes cold and dark
But theres not always an easy path
As with a blind cupids arrow missing the mark

I suddenly stopped in my tracks
I seen you standing there but did you not notice me
I begin to feel my self sinking quicksand beneath my feet
I look again to you but my trouble you did not see

With each pull i reach for your help
Each time the quicksand grips tightens below
I feel the heartbreaks of the past taking hold
Just one glimpse is all you need for it to truely show

When i reach the bottom will it be the end
Will love be my true strength my words asscend
Alone i slip beneath perhaps this is my fate
Just when it gets dark theres light mine in your hand

Fate has taking its time your love was my final hope
All along you too tried to hide what you truely felt inside
Now together no more quicksand is in our path
The solid ground our future one that no longer needs to
hide

FireProof

From the start love can seem to hide
Longer it stays hidden the more it shall be
Once revealed it can open so many doors
Then one or two shall feel and open hearts see

To love someone is to develop a strong bond
We each follow the one were with no matter the bringing
Love one another just as gods love is shown to us all
For true unconditional love can be transforming

Along the way sometimes one looks for the flaws
Some may be found but blessings are there as well
The passion burns In the heat of our everlasting flames
For without love without heart then all sure is to fail

Love isnt always quick nor is it fireproof
The flames are always destined to come to it
We can prepare ourselves for when they do
So that what is can be strong to withstand it
Then this will be a true reflection for all to see
The final test comes when you say the words I Do
Time will lift your strengths to continue not give up
The Commitment that was made for life this is true

Marriage is a sacred bond one that can last forever
Now it may seem not to burn out but its not always
fireproof
Both have to go with what comes thru thick and thin
With faith then one can conquer anything with love as
proof

Another Chance around

Things in the past many times ive done wrong
Decisons i know could have done differant
Times choices were weak when my heart wasnt strong
Signals from within werent always sent

Never before was there another as you
Feelings kept in hold many never let go
I now see the words i should have said
The things that that was meant now know

More than miles seemed between us
One thing that inside i always knew to be
Was the way you made me feel when together
After it was was gone is when i truely could see

We can not bring back things of the past
Nor can we know what the future will hold
Today can be the start the place to start something new
With the heat of love we can break from the lonley cold

For fate perhaps gives us this day the other chance
One more time for our hearts to melt within a kiss
Things may have changed but who cares where it will lead
Cause for if not for this it will always be you i surely miss

The Poets Pen

Here sits a poet alone with words of his soul
Picking up a pen writes feelings from within
Past heartaches to future dreams making one whole
Looking to share his life with someone again

The words flowed out like a mighty river
Hope love and romance burned like raging fires
With the help of his pen what lines would it deliever
Would the mere lines show what he truely desires

With each new poem a little more of him was shown
Expressed deep emotions in some happy times in other
Then there were the hidden feelings the he had only known
The will to keep going fueled by the waiting of another

Many a time these poems were guiding hands for some
And they were future inspirations for many more
For the poet they were life and the patience to come
One true message stood out in all true love he was waiting
for

Nothing lasts forever all good things do come to an end
So to the hope that the one dreamed of soon by his side
Bring new life to a tired heart breath new life from his pen
Share the truths feelings with someone where need not hide

But now near the end fear grows these words may soon end
Then the poet will be again more alone lost from within
Maybe never truely able to tell another or know his angel
did send
The time will soon come when the ink will run out of his
pen

Burning candle of the Heart

Light this candle within your heart
You see sometimes things happen the flame goes out
If true love is there meant to be then its strong from the
start
The flame will overcome any thing no matter what about

But from within the darkness comes the ultimate test
Thru life the heart finds the ups and downs thrown its way
For then the love built with each now stands at its best
The flame may flicker but for now its kept the darkness at
bay

Honesty Trust and Truths bind together the shield that
holds it back
For not always can just one keep it bright and always lit
The combining of two souls as one protect from any attack
True love now fuels the flame love now here truly fit
The Light of life always keeping one out of the dark
The candle burning to fight the despair and the pain
Then along comes hope always with it will hit its mark
So without love a lone mind can feel cold feel like going
insane

With the souls of two this flame burning tall and bright
Blocking out the dark and with it a cold heart warm by its
heat
So no matter what fight this flame can always remain day
into the darkest night
So with true love open heart and honest souls can one keep
lit the flame lifes true feat

Timeless Wanderer

Walking the path of life alone
Walked for all time looking for the one
My thoughts and the voices heard were my own
Just a simple soul a single heart looking to be reborn

Not till the day i saw you
Was my search just a mere dream
Would the one at the end of this journey feel it to
Perhaps what i saw in you was just a mere faint gleam

Walking alone i seemed to at times lose my way
I had no map had no compass just the thought of you
Guided me when i felt lost and the closing light of day
Never a time to stop to rest not till things were shown true

Maybe god will send me the sign from above
For then my heart will know its ready for another
For then ill know what it will be to feel true love
So for now my journey continues as the timeless wanderer

Behind these Falls

The rivers flow just as the words i write flow from within
Each time changing itself and all that it show
Where one stops another few words reach out to begin
For its one of many ways for others to see feelings and to
know

The words keep pushing on like the might river
Each line written as the river carries onward
Pushing forth to something new not once slowing up never
This progress each day and what keeps it moving forward

Over a majestic mountain side it moves down ever so fast
To the bottom of the mountain side crashing the rocks
below
A fine mist fills the air but the river continues its quest
Will this journey come to its end no one truely know

With the viewing of this magnificent sight of nature
One knows its never an option to give up on what is yet to
be
You see the waterfall covers a hidden cave one with a
certain feature
Deep within the realms lies a loving soul looking to be set
free

Held back by time looking to burst forth
Hidden ready to be awaken freed from these walls
Then the true beginning shall be seen in all its worth
So as the river flows on what remains is something much
more behind these falls